Scars and Storms

27 Principles for a Life Worth Living

By Joseph Babcock

Disclaimer

This book offers personal insights and strategies for resilience based on lived experience. While these principles have proven helpful, they are not intended as professional counseling, medical advice, or treatment for mental health conditions. Every person's journey through adversity is unique, and healing isn't always linear.

If you're experiencing persistent depression, anxiety, trauma, or thoughts of self-harm, please consult qualified mental health professionals. Some storms require professional support alongside personal resilience practices.

The wisdom in these pages is meant to complement, not replace, appropriate professional care when needed.

Dedication

To SJ, whose authentic spirit and genuine heart reminded me that wisdom earned through struggle deserves to be shared, lighting the way forward and inspiring these words. Your friendship was a gift.

Acknowledgments

To my parents, Joseph and Dolores - whose unwavering love and support showed me what strength looks like in action.

To Danielle and Joey - being your father has taught me more about love, patience, and growth than any book could. Our challenges have made us all stronger. I love you both.

To my siblings Lorie, Margy, Danny and Michael - our bond has been my anchor through every storm.

To Dr. Ryan Hosely - whose integrity as both friend and professional showed me what it means to build a life on solid principles.

To Alan Koloen, a mentor and friend whose guidance, wisdom, and unwavering support have been instrumental in my journey. I'm grateful for the bond we've formed, and I look forward to our ongoing connection.

To Dan Martell - Your book Buy Back Your Time came at the right moment when I was burning out. It motivated me to shift gears, reclaim focus, and build a life that actually works. It changed my trajectory.

To those who taught me hard lessons through difficult seasons - the wisdom came through the pain, not despite it.

To every reader walking through their own storm - your courage to keep building inspires this work.

A Letter to You from the Author

Dear Reader,

The best things in life are gifts. Things like breathing, having hope, and getting a second chance to start over.

Ideas are gifts, too.

That's what *Scars and Storms* is: a toolbox of ideas you can use in real life—especially when things get tough.

I could have made this book 270 pages long. I didn't. I kept it short on purpose. I want you to be able to read it fast, understand it easily, and **put it to work** right away.

So, here is my question:

Will you try it?

Just one principle. One day at a time. That is how you survive a storm. That is how your scars become wisdom instead of just old wounds.

If this book helps you, please don't keep it to yourself.

Give it to a friend who is struggling. Pass it on to someone who needs a win. Leave a note inside and give it away.

There is a simple law in life: **you get by giving.**

—The Author

Preface

Life doesn't shape us in comfort—it shapes us in storms. The scars I carry are not marks of failure but lessons of survival. Adversity is the forge that makes us stronger, more capable, and ready for whatever comes next.

Not every storm teaches the same lessons, and not everyone heals at the same pace. Some wounds take longer to transform into wisdom. That's part of being human.

Introduction

Storms come in family, health, relationships, and work. None of us escape them. What separates those who break from those who build is simple: perspective. This book weaves ancient wisdom, Stoic philosophy, and transformative thinking into a framework for resilience—practical, story-driven, and anchored in real life.

Adversity doesn't diminish us; it prepares us. Every challenge faced can make you more equipped for the next one. These 27 principles will help you transform your storms into strength. But remember - healing isn't a race, and some storms may require professional support alongside personal resilience.

Author Visionary Statement

I am a scarred builder, not an academic. My voice comes from storms endured and scars carried. Discipline, faith, and perspective turn wounds into wisdom. Adversity has been my greatest teacher—showing me that what doesn't destroy you can indeed make you ready for what's next.

But I've also learned that strength doesn't always look the same for everyone, and sometimes the bravest thing is asking for help.

Table of Contents

Chapter 1:
Gratitude in the Storm

Opening Question

When storms hit—in health, family, or work—do you see only what's been torn away, or do you notice what's still standing?

Story

Gratitude is easy when life feels good. But when you're staring at broken relationships, failed plans, or regrets from bad choices, gratitude feels impossible. And yet, that's when it matters most.

Gratitude doesn't erase scars. It teaches you how to carry them. I've watched people walk through crisis—some got bitter, others stronger. The difference wasn't the storm; it was their perspective. Gratitude is not denial. It's defiance. It says: This storm won't decide who I become.

Every storm you survive makes you more capable of weathering the next one. Gratitude in adversity builds the muscle memory of resilience.

Ancient Teaching

"Give thanks in all circumstances; this is wisdom's way."

Stoic Echo

Seneca: "He is a wise man who does not grieve for the things which he has not, but rejoices for those which he has."

Balance Principle

Balance: Obsessing over lack creates imbalance. Lower the pressure; balance returns; new opportunities appear.

Dialogue Prompts
- When has adversity blinded you to blessings still present?
- What do you have now that you once prayed for?
- How might gratitude shift how you see today's struggles?

Daily Practice
Write three hard things and one gift hidden in each. Thank someone—or the universe—for what remains.

Chapter 2:
Worthy of Love

Opening Question
Do your scars make you feel unworthy of love—or more prepared to give and receive it?

Story
Family crises, broken relationships, or bad decisions often leave you feeling unworthy. Adversity whispers: "You're too damaged. No one could love you now." But scars are not proof you're unworthy. They're proof you've lived.

Love isn't for the flawless. It's for the real. Every broken place in your life can either become a wall that shuts others out, or a doorway that lets love in. Being worthy of love doesn't mean being perfect—it means accepting your humanity, learning from failure, and showing up honestly.

The storms that wounded you also equipped you to love others through their storms. Your scars become your credentials for compassion. Some people heal faster than others—that doesn't make anyone less worthy.

Ancient Teaching
"True love is shown not when we are perfect, but while we are still flawed."

Stoic Echo
Epictetus: Wish events to unfold as they do; acceptance precedes action and opens space for love.

Balance Principle
Balance: Chasing love with desperation creates resistance. Stand whole and the right love finds you.

Dialogue Prompts

- What past failure makes you feel unworthy of love?
- Who convinced you that scars make you less?
- What would change if you saw your scars as proof of survival, not disqualification?

Daily Practice

Mirror exercise: say aloud, "I am worthy of love, scars and all." Repeat until it lands.

Chapter 3:
Happiness Is Your Responsibility

Opening Question
Whose shoulders are you placing your happiness on—yours, or someone else's?

Story
Adversity exposes this lie: "If they loved me more, if my job treated me better, if life was fairer, then I'd be happy." That mindset is a trap. If your happiness depends on people or circumstances, it will always collapse when storms hit.

Owning your happiness doesn't mean ignoring pain. It means refusing to hand over the keys to your peace. Bad bosses, broken families, failed ventures—they can wound you, yes. But they don't get to define your joy. Happiness is built from inside, not delivered from outside.

Each disappointment that forces you to find joy within makes you less dependent on the world's approval. Adversity teaches self-reliance in the most important area: your inner peace.

Ancient Teaching
"True strength comes from inner joy that no external force can steal."

Stoic Echo
Marcus Aurelius: "Very little is needed to make a happy life; it is all within yourself."

Balance Principle
Balance: Clinging to external conditions creates imbalance; shift inward and balance returns.

Dialogue Prompts

- Who have you been holding responsible for your happiness?
- How has adversity revealed the danger of outsourcing your joy?
- What small choice could you make today that's only for your peace?

Daily Practice

Choose one small joy today that's only for you—not to impress anyone.

Chapter 4:
Breaking Free from People-Pleasing

Opening Question
Where does the need to please others steal your peace most—home, friends, or work?

Story
People-pleasing feels kind—until it erases you. I learned this in small betrayals: saying yes when I meant no, fixing messes I didn't make, and smiling through resentment. Storms exposed it. When a crisis hit, my 'nice' habits crumbled; honesty was the only bridge that held.

Freedom began when I stopped auditioning for approval. Some people left. The ones who stayed met the real me.

The hardest lessons about boundaries come through pain. But each time you choose truth over approval, you become stronger and more authentic.

Adversity burns away the false self.

Ancient Teaching
"Fear of others' judgment becomes a trap that binds the soul."

Stoic Echo
Stoic: Prefer what is up to you; ignore what isn't.

Balance Principle
Balance: Stop overvaluing approval; energy returns to you instead of feeding the 'pendulum.'

Dialogue Prompts
- Where are you saying yes but meaning no?
- Which relationship needs a boundary stated plainly?
- What quiet act would prove you choose truth over approval?

Daily Practice
Say one honest no today. No apology. No long defense. Just a clean, respectful no.

Chapter 5:
Loving Others As They Are

Opening Question
Can you love people as they are without trying to change them?

Story
I thought I was helping people by trying to fix them. I used to 'help' by correcting, fixing, and nudging. It only tightened knots. When I learned to accept people as they are, conversations softened. Oddly, change came faster—because it wasn't demanded.

Love is not a lever; it's a presence. The more I released control, the more room others had to rise.

My own struggles with being controlled taught me the gift of acceptance. The pain of feeling judged made me slower to judge. Adversity creates better lovers.

Ancient Teaching
"Bear with one another; forgiveness heals what force cannot."

Stoic Echo
Marcus: People act from their own reasons—meet them with justice.

Balance Principle
Balance: Lower importance. Allow others to be as they are; friction drops.

Dialogue Prompts
- Who are you trying to 'improve'?
- What would acceptance look like this week?
- Where can you trade fixing for listening?

Daily Practice

Practice listening without correction for one whole conversation. Reflect later—what changed?

Chapter 6:
Energy That Attracts

Opening Question
What signal are you broadcasting in the room before you speak?

Story
Some rooms felt heavy until I walked in calmly and refused to match the chaos. That taught me this: energy communicates faster than words. When I carried anger, conflict found me. When I carried steadiness, even tense meetings cooled.

Your presence is a thermostat, not a thermometer. Set it on purpose.

Learning to control your energy comes through weathering storms that could have broken your spirit. Each crisis you handle with grace makes you a calmer force in the next one.

Ancient Teaching
"A peaceful heart brings healing like medicine."

Stoic Echo
Seneca: We attract what our mind dwells upon.

Balance Principle
Balance: Radiate calm intention; like attracts like in balanced fields.

Dialogue Prompts
- Where do you mirror chaos you could calm?
- What would a calmer version of you do in that room?
- What pre-meeting ritual keeps you steady?

Daily Practice

Before your next hard conversation, breathe for 60 seconds, drop your shoulders, and picture a peaceful outcome.

Chapter 7:
Mind, Body, and Spirit Alignment

Opening Question
Where is your body arguing with your beliefs?

Story
I could preach discipline while sleeping four hours and living on caffeine. The storm that hit my health forced a reckoning. Mind, body, and spirit aren't separate silos; they're one system. When I slept, stretched, and meditated, my patience returned—and so did my clarity.

Alignment isn't flashy. It's meals, movement, and meaning, repeated.

Health crises teach what lectures cannot: your body keeps the score. The discipline you build recovering from breakdown makes you stronger than you were before the fall. But remember—some health challenges require medical support, not just willpower.

Ancient Teaching
"Honor the temple of your being with care and reverence."

Stoic Echo
Epictetus: Train body, mind, and will together.

Balance Principle
Balance: Balanced inner state reduces wild swings; health choices stabilize the field.

Dialogue Prompts

- Which habit wrecks your sleep or focus?
- What 15-minute routine would shift your day?
- Who can walk this with you for accountability?

Daily Practice

Pick one: bedtime alarm, 10-minute stretch, or a 15-minute walk. Do it daily for seven days.

Chapter 8:
Dream, Visualize, Feel

Opening Question
Are you seeing the future you want—and feeling it as if it's here?

Story
When I only 'hoped,' nothing moved. When I pictured the goal, felt it in my bones, and took one step daily, doors opened. Visualization isn't magic; it's rehearsal. Your body learns the path your mind walks first.

You have to believe it in order to see it.

Feel it, then do the next small thing.

Dreams forged in the fire of adversity have a different quality—they're born from necessity, not fantasy. The clearer your vision becomes through struggle, the more power it has to pull you forward.

Ancient Teaching
"Write the vision clearly; make it plain for all to see."

Stoic Echo
Marcus: The soul becomes dyed with the color of its thoughts.

Balance Principle
Balance: Feel the scene fulfilled; lower importance; let life arrange the steps.

Dialogue Prompts
- What do you want to see in 90 days?
- What does it feel like when you've lived it?
- What is the next 10-minute action?

Daily Practice

Spend 5 minutes visualizing your outcome, then immediately complete a 10-minute related action.

Chapter 9:
Ask, Believe, Receive

Opening Question
Do you ask boldly, believe steadily, and receive without clutching?

Story
I used to ask like I was bargaining. Faith grew when I asked clearly, worked faithfully, and stopped grabbing. Receiving isn't passivity; it's readiness. I learned to keep my hands open—not tight.

You can't pick up new tools with clenched fists.

Desperation makes you grab; adversity survived with grace makes you ready to receive. The difference is everything.

Ancient Teaching
"Ask and it will be given; seek and you will find."

Stoic Echo
Stoic: Ask for the right use of events, not the events themselves.

Balance Principle
Balance: Intend lightly; act simply; let outcomes land without strain.

Dialogue Prompts
- Where do you ask vaguely?
- What would a clear, specific ask look like?
- How will you recognize the answer when it arrives?

Daily Practice

Write one precise request today (email, intention, or proposal). Send it.

Chapter 10:
Confidence as a Compass

Opening Question
When did you last act confident before you felt confident?

Story
Confidence didn't arrive; I built it. First in small rooms, then bigger ones. I kept promises to myself, stacked tiny wins, and let results speak louder than nerves.

Confidence isn't noise. It's consistency measured over time.

Luck is for the unprepared.

Real confidence comes from surviving what you thought would break you. Each storm weathered adds another layer of "I can handle this" to your core.

Ancient Teaching
"Be strong and of good courage; let your heart be firm."

Stoic Echo
Seneca: Fortune favors the prepared.

Balance Principle
Balance: Decisive, low-importance moves open doors.

Dialogue Prompts
- Which promise to yourself needs to be kept this week?
- What skill will you practice for 20 minutes today?
- Where can you let results speak instead of arguing?

Daily Practice

Choose one promise to keep for seven days. Track it in writing.

Chapter 11:
Owning Your Story

Opening Question
What's the story you tell about yourself—and who wrote it?

Story
For years I carried a script I didn't author: the fixer, the tough one, the quiet mule that hauls the weight. Storms tore pages out. I wrote new ones. Owning your story doesn't mean glorifying pain; it means telling the truth about it so it stops owning you.

Write it, don't relive it.

The power to rewrite your narrative comes through facing what actually happened. Adversity strips away the comfortable lies and forces you to deal with reality. That's where real authorship begins.

Ancient Teaching
"Confess your faults to one another, that healing may come."

Stoic Echo
Marcus: Blame no one; own your part.

Balance Principle
Balance: Let go of what weighs you down; alignment restores flow.

Dialogue Prompts
- What label do you want to retire?
- What truth do you need to say out loud?
- Who hears your new story first?

Daily Practice

Write one page titled 'The Story I Choose Now.' Read it aloud.

Chapter 12:
Mastering Your Emotions

Opening Question
What emotion runs your day—and do you run it back?

Story
Anger drove a season of my life. It fueled me—and then it created damage I had to repair. I had to recognize the warning signs before I lost control. When I started breathing through anger and redirecting it instead of unleashing it, I saved relationships I thought were over. Mastery isn't suppression; it's choosing what it becomes.

Feel it fully. Choose what it becomes.

Emotional mastery is forged in the fires of loss and disappointment. Each time you choose response over reaction, you become more capable of handling the next emotional storm. Some deep wounds may need professional support to heal properly.

Ancient Teaching
"Be slow to anger and rich in compassion."

Stoic Echo
Epictetus: If provoked, pause and count the cost.

Balance Principle
Balance: Lower importance; emotions settle; clarity returns.

Dialogue Prompts
- What emotion shows up most?
- How does it protect you—and hurt you?
- What 90-second reset will you try today?

Daily Practice

Use a 90-second breath reset twice today when emotion spikes.

Chapter 13:
Living in Integrity

Opening Question
When did you last do the right thing with no audience?

Story
Integrity is built offstage. I learned this through small compromises - taking shortcuts when no one was watching, committing to more than I could realistically handle, or choosing the easier path when I knew better was required. Storms expose foundations. Doing what's right—especially when it costs—quiets the mind and strengthens the spine.

Your future self spends the dividends.

The small compromises that seem harmless become the weak points where you break under pressure. Adversity tests every shortcut you've taken and every corner you've cut.

Ancient Teaching
"Let your yes be yes, and your no be no; integrity needs no ornament."

Stoic Echo
Marcus: If it isn't right, don't do it.

Balance Principle
Balance: Integrity stabilizes the field; results compound.

Dialogue Prompts
- Where is your word wobbly?
- Which small honesty will you practice today?
- What standard will you not negotiate?

Daily Practice

Choose one integrity action (refund, apology, correction) and do it today.

Chapter 14:
Respecting Opinions, Guarding Peace

Opening Question
Are you protecting your peace—or debating it away online and at dinner?

Story
I mistook arguing for influence. I'd jump into debates at work, convinced my colleagues needed to hear the truth. I was often right, but that didn't matter when people started avoiding me with their problems. At family dinners, I'd correct relatives' political opinions, convinced I was educating them. It only fed the noise and turned family gatherings into tension zones. Peace came when I learned to let opinions pass by like weather. Not every remark deserves your energy. Save your strength for real work.

Silence can be leadership.

Learning what fights are worth having comes through losing battles that didn't matter. Each pointless argument teaches you to guard your energy for what actually counts.

Ancient Teaching
"As far as it depends on you, live at peace with all."

Stoic Echo
Seneca: Opinions aren't facts; don't rent them your mind.

Balance Principle
Balance: De-energize needless debates; balance returns.

Dialogue Prompts

- Which conversation drains you every time?
- What boundary sentence will you use next time?
- Where will you stay silent on purpose?

Daily Practice

Practice one polite exit line: "I'm not discussing this today." Use it once.

Chapter 15:
Thoughts Shape Reality

Opening Question
What thought pattern keeps replaying—and what is it producing?

Story
When I believed I was always behind schedule, behind others, behind where I should be, I rushed through decisions and relationships, cutting corners on projects and interrupting conversations to prove my point. I broke more than I fixed - damaging connections, making costly mistakes that set me back even further. When I believed I could learn and grow at my own pace, I slowed down, asked questions, listened to what people actually needed, and made thoughtful choices that built a more solid foundation. Thoughts are not decorations; they are blueprints. Change the pattern, change the structure.

Guard your inner architect.

Adversity reveals the thoughts that have been quietly building your reality. The crisis that breaks you also shows you which mental patterns need to be rebuilt stronger.

Ancient Teaching
"As a person thinks in their heart, so they become."

Stoic Echo
Marcus: The mind shapes reality.

Balance Principle
Balance: Where attention goes, energy flows; outcomes follow.

Dialogue Prompts
- What thought shows up daily?
- What fruit has it produced?
- What truth will you rehearse instead?

Daily Practice

Write one replacement thought on a card. Read it morning and night for seven days.

Chapter 16:
Take Action, Build Momentum

Opening Question
What action would make tomorrow meaningfully different—
and can you do it in 10 minutes?

Story
Momentum beats motivation. I'd sit paralyzed by all the things
I should do, waiting for the energy or perfect conditions to tackle
them. The pile grew while I waited for Monday, or motivation, or
the perfect plan. I learned to move when I didn't feel like it - pick
one small thing and just begin, even badly. Ten minutes became
thirty, and thirty became finished. Waiting for perfect wiped
years. Moving imperfectly built a life.

Do the smallest true thing. Then another.

Action becomes easier when you've survived seasons of
paralysis. Each time you move through fear and resistance, you
build the muscle memory of courage.

Ancient Teaching
"Whatever your hand finds to do, do it with all your might."

Stoic Echo
Epictetus: Decide who you will be, then do the deeds.

Balance Principle
Balance: Action collapses probability into reality.

Dialogue Prompts
- What's your smallest true action?
- Where will you place it on the calendar?
- How will you lower the friction to start?

Daily Practice

Do one 10-minute action now. Set a daily repeating reminder.

Chapter 17:
Courage as Daily Fuel

Opening Question
What would courage look like in the next hour—not the next year?

Story
Courage isn't fireworks; it's phone calls you've been avoiding, applications that feel like long shots, and honest 'no more' when you're being taken advantage of. I practiced courage in daily doses - one scary conversation, one uncomfortable email, one boundary that felt risky to hold. The fear stayed; I moved anyway.

Small brave acts change trajectories.

Courage is built one small step at a time through adversity. Each fear faced makes the next one less intimidating. Bravery compounds.

Ancient Teaching
"Take heart; be of good courage."

Stoic Echo
Seneca: Sometimes even to live is an act of courage.

Balance Principle
Balance: Balanced intention reduces fear's pull; move lightly.

Dialogue Prompts
- What scares you in a useful way?
- What's the 5-minute brave step?
- Who will you tell after you do it?

Daily Practice

Take one five-minute brave action before the day ends. Log it.

Chapter 18:
Power of Imagination

Opening Question
What future are you rehearsing in your mind every day?

Story
Imagination is a tool, not an escape. For years I used it to rehearse disaster - picturing business meetings going wrong, relationships failing, health problems spiraling out of control. I was an expert at mental catastrophizing across every area of life. Turning it toward possibility felt awkward at first - visualizing success seemed like setting myself up for disappointment. But when I started imagining positive outcomes in my work, relationships, and personal challenges, then taking action toward them, it became a lever. See it, feel it, act.

Direct the projector.

The imagination trained by adversity has different power—it's grounded in reality, not fantasy. You can envision better because you've seen worse and survived it.

Ancient Teaching
"All growth comes from the seed of imagination planted well."

Stoic Echo
Marcus: The imagination has power—aim it.

Balance Principle
Balance: Imagine lightly; avoid importance; allow movement.

Dialogue Prompts
- What picture are you replaying lately?
- What would a healthier picture be?
- What action pairs with that picture today?

Daily Practice
Spend 3 minutes on a positive scene, then complete one linked action.

Chapter 19:
Choosing Humility

Opening Question
Where does pride keep you from learning the very lesson you
need?

Story
    Humility let me grow faster than talent ever did. I used to think
I knew more than I actually did, politely declining offers for
additional training or coaching. I would argue points in
conversations, needing to prove I was right about everything.
When I dropped my guard and started engaging with mentors and
coaches, admitting my mistakes openly, feedback landed and
relationships deepened. Pride kept me isolated; humility made me
useful.

    Stay teachable, especially when you're tired.

    Pride gets humbled by life eventually. You can choose humility
or have it chosen for you. Choosing it yourself hurts less and
teaches more.

Ancient Teaching
    "Humble yourself, and you will be lifted up in due time."

Stoic Echo
    Epictetus: Be a student first.

Balance Principle
    Balance: Release over-importance; flow returns.

Dialogue Prompts
- What feedback are you resisting?
- Who could you ask for help today?
- What mistake will you admit without a story?

Daily Practice

Ask one person for specific feedback. Write down their answer without defending.

Chapter 20:
Losing the Inflated Ego

Opening Question
What has your ego cost you recently—a friendship, a client, a night's sleep?

Story
My ego loved being right more than being wise. I'd spend meetings focused on proving my point rather than solving problems, turn family conversations into battles I had to win, and engage in political arguments with strangers at social gatherings. At work, I'd win debates but miss collaborative opportunities. At home, I'd correct every mistake and need the last word. In social settings, I couldn't let opposing viewpoints pass without challenge. It won arguments and lost people. The day I let go of needing to win every discussion, solutions arrived faster at work, connections deepened at home, and social interactions became enjoyable again. The work spoke for itself.

Deflate the balloon before it pops.

Life has a way of deflating inflated egos through adversity. The harder the fall, the more painful the lesson. Better to step down voluntarily than be knocked down inevitably.

Ancient Teaching
"Pride comes before a fall; arrogance before destruction."

Stoic Echo
Marcus: Vanity is noise; cut it.

Balance Principle
Balance: Deflate importance; regain balance and clarity.

Dialogue Prompts

- Where are you reacting to protect your image, not principle?
- What would quiet confidence choose here?
- Who deserves an un-defensive check-in?

Daily Practice

Pick one ego-fueled situation. Choose silence or service instead of defense.

Chapter 21:
Freedom from Others' Opinions

Opening Question
How much is other people's opinion costing your peace?

Story
When I stopped treating opinions like court verdicts, I started sleeping. I used to lie awake replaying workplace criticism, analyzing every comment from colleagues, letting their feedback control my mood for days. I'd obsess over what people thought about my decisions—where I lived, how I spent money, what I chose to do with my time. I'd replay every family dinner conversation, worrying about disappointing my parents or my kids, letting their concerns about my choices consume my thoughts. Approval is wind—it shifts. Purpose is an anchor—it holds. You can hear feedback without surrendering your steering wheel.

Choose your true north and walk it calmly.

Freedom from opinion comes through having them not matter when you needed them most. When you've walked alone through your darkest valley, crowd approval loses its grip.

Ancient Teaching
"We must follow higher truth rather than popular opinion."

Stoic Echo
Stoic: Other people's opinions are indifferent.

Balance Principle
Balance: Stop feeding the approval pendulum; energy returns to purpose.

Dialogue Prompts
- What decision have you delayed due to imagined criticism?
- What one sentence summarizes your purpose here?
- What boundary ends the drift?

Daily Practice
Write your purpose sentence. Put it on your lock screen for a week.

Chapter 22:
Persistence Against Resistance

Opening Question
Where do you stop when resistance shows up—and what if you didn't?

Story
Everything worthwhile met resistance: rebuilding trust after damaging relationships, learning new skills when I felt too old to start over, making amends when pride wanted me to stay silent. Pursuing opportunities that seemed beyond my experience, rebuilding after financial setbacks, early morning workouts when my body wanted sleep, difficult conversations I'd been avoiding for months. I used to read resistance as a stop sign—if people pushed back or it felt uncomfortable, I'd retreat. Now I read it as a mile marker showing I'm moving toward something that matters.

Keep walking—especially when it isn't glamorous.

Persistence through adversity builds different muscle than persistence through comfort. When you've kept going through real pain, ordinary resistance becomes manageable.

Ancient Teaching
"Do not grow weary in doing good; the harvest will come."

Stoic Echo
Seneca: Persist and you conquer.

Balance Principle
Balance: Consistency reduces resistance; results compound.

Dialogue Prompts
- Where did you quit last time?
- What minimum viable daily action keeps you moving?
- Who will you report progress to weekly?

Daily Practice

Commit to a 'no zero days' streak for seven days. Record one line each night.

Chapter 23:
Gratitude Revisited

Opening Question
What new blessings did your latest storm make possible?

Story
Gratitude looks different after you've bled. It becomes practical: family members who forgave your mistakes, moments of peace after months of chaos. A friend who calls to check in, friends who stayed in touch when others disappeared, a working truck that gets you to the job site, a roof over your head when you thought you might lose it, waking up grateful for another day when you wondered if you'd see it. Returning to gratitude isn't naïve; it's strategic. It keeps your heart from hardening.

Gratitude again. And again.

The gratitude forged in fire burns brighter than the gratitude born in comfort.

What seems ordinary to others looks miraculous to eyes that have seen loss.

Ancient Teaching
"In all things, give thanks; this is wisdom's way."

Stoic Echo
Marcus: Rehearse gratitude daily.

Balance Principle
Balance: Gratitude lowers excess potential; life synchronizes.

Dialogue Prompts
- What three ordinary goods carried you this week?
- Who deserves a thank-you note?
- How does gratitude change today's decisions?

Daily Practice

Send one short thank-you message today. Write two more tomorrow.

Chapter 24:
Humility in Relationships

Opening Question
What would humility look like in your nearest relationship today?

Story
Humility doesn't mean disappearing. It means choosing the relationship over being right. I used to approach conversations with partners as problems to solve rather than people to understand, always having the better solution instead of listening to their actual concerns. I'd also correct my kids constantly, turning every conversation into a teaching moment instead of just connecting with them. It took meeting someone whose genuine spirit showed me a different way - that relationships thrive on acceptance, not correction. When I finally learned to step down from the podium in my mind, I began to hear what I'd missed with my children—their actual feelings and concerns—and am working towards the closeness I want.

Humility is the shortest path back to connection.

Relationships that survive adversity teach you what matters: connection over correction, presence over performance. The arguments you thought were important fade next to the people who stayed.

Ancient Teaching
"Clothe yourselves with humility toward one another."

Stoic Echo
Epictetus: Serve where you stand.

Balance Principle

Balance: Choose low importance in conflict; connection returns.

Dialogue Prompts

- Where are you performing instead of relating?
- What apology or admission would open a door?
- What generous assumption can you make today?

Daily Practice

Do one quiet act of service for someone close—unannounced, unposted.

Chapter 25:
Joy in Everyday Moments

Opening Question
What small joy are you overlooking in the rush to 'fix everything'?

Story
Some days joy was coffee in a chipped mug before the house woke up, the quiet satisfaction of fixing something that was broken, catching a sunrise on the drive to work. A text from one of my kids just to say hello, completing a project that had been hanging over my head, or a brief conversation with someone who understood what I was going through. The smell of fresh lumber on a job site, watching rain wash the dust off everything, making progress on something I'd been putting off for months, or learning a skill that had intimidated me. When I counted small joys, big problems shrank to size. Joy isn't ignoring pain; it's noticing light where it still shows up.

Joy restores courage to keep building.

Loss teaches you to treasure what remains. The small joys that others take for granted become precious when you've known their absence. Adversity sharpens your appreciation.

Ancient Teaching
"Rejoice always; find joy in each moment given."

Stoic Echo
Marcus: Joy is a decision of the ruling faculty.

Balance Principle
Balance: Joy is balanced energy; it attracts ease.

Dialogue Prompts
- Where did joy appear today already?
- What joy could you schedule for 15 minutes?
- Who lifts your spirit—and when will you call them?

Daily Practice
List five small joys. Do one today before noon.

Chapter 26:
Apologies and True Change

Opening Question
What apology would mean something—words plus change?

Story
I apologized with explanations for years. When I missed deadlines, I'd explain all the reasons why instead of simply taking responsibility. When I hurt my kids or family members, I'd explain my stress, my circumstances - everything except acknowledging the real harm I'd caused. Every time I disappointed someone, I'd follow 'I'm sorry' with 'but' and a list of reasons why it wasn't entirely my fault. It never healed anything. Real apologies are short and followed by repair. When I changed the behavior, trust returned slowly—but it returned.

Let your actions finish your sentences.

An apology without change is just manipulation.

The best apologies come from people who've been broken by their own mistakes. Rock bottom gives you the motivation to rebuild differently.

Adversity creates authentic repentance.

Ancient Teaching
"Bear fruit that proves your change of heart."

Stoic Echo
Seneca: Don't just complain—amend your life.

Balance Principle
Balance: Shift from importance to action; prove change.

Dialogue Prompts

- Who have you hurt?
- What action would repair a small part of the harm?
- When will you do it?

Daily Practice

Make one concrete amends within 48 hours—money, time, or changed habit.

Chapter 27:
Hope Anchored in Faith

Opening Question
What do you anchor to when nothing moves and the night is long?

Story
Hope isn't a wish; it's a quiet decision to keep walking when outcomes aren't visible. I have lived nights like that—staring at photos of my kids wondering if I'd ever repair what I'd damaged, sitting in empty rooms that used to be full of family, fear louder than faith. Financial statements spread across the table showing losses, phone calls that didn't come through, medical reports that scared me, facing changes I never saw coming. Anchor to what does not move, then take the next step.

Morning comes.

Ancient Teaching
"Hope is the anchor of the soul, firm and secure."

Stoic Echo
Marcus: Look to what remains in your control.

Balance Principle
Balance: Hope is a calm intention—balanced, not desperate.

Dialogue Prompts
- Where do you need an anchor tonight?
- What is the next small step regardless of feelings?
- Who will you text for support?

Daily Practice
Write tomorrow's first step on a sticky note and place it on your phone.

Final Reflection

Every scar tells a story. Every storm offers a choice. Adversity doesn't diminish you—it prepares you for what's next. Turn storms into strength, one honest practice at a time.

The person you become through weathering life's storms is stronger, wiser, and more capable than the person who never faced them. Your scars are not your shame; they are your credentials.

Remember: healing isn't a race. Some storms require time, support, and professional help. That doesn't make you weak—it makes you wise.

Connect with the Author

Joseph Babcock continues building, writing, and helping others transform their storms into strength.

Email: 27principles@proton.me

For speaking engagements, workshops, or to share your own storm-to-strength story, reach out. Every scar has wisdom worth sharing.

About the Author

Joseph Babcock is a scarred builder forged in adversity. His background spans leadership, manufacturing, and construction. His guiding principle: *scars don't disqualify you; they qualify you.*

Through personal storms and professional challenges, he has learned that adversity isn't the enemy of strength—it's the forge where strength is made. This book represents decades of hard-won wisdom about turning wounds into wisdom and storms into steps forward.

Final Note to Readers

If you're struggling with thoughts of self-harm, persistent depression, or trauma that feels overwhelming, please reach out to mental health professionals, trusted friends, or crisis helplines in your area.

These principles work best alongside appropriate support when needed. Your life has value, your story matters, and help is available.

United States:
National Crisis Text Line: Text HOME to 741741
National Suicide Prevention Lifeline: 988

Canada:
9-8-8: Suicide Crisis Helpline: Call or text 9-8-8
Kids Help Phone: 1-800-668-6868 or text CONNECT to 686868

United Kingdom:
Samaritans: 116 123 (24/7 helpline)
Text SHOUT to 85258 (crisis text line)

Australia:
Lifeline: 13 11 14 (24/7 crisis support)
Beyond Blue: 1300 22 4636

New Zealand:
Lifeline Aotearoa: 0800 543 354
Suicide Crisis Helpline: 0508 828 865 (0508 TAUTOKO)

España (Spain):
Teléfono de la Esperanza: 717 003 717
Teléfono contra el Suicidio: 911 385 385

For other countries, search for local crisis support in your area.